THE FIFTH SUN

by

NICHOLAS A. PATRICCA

The Dramatic Publishing Company
Woodstock, Illinois • London, England • Melbourne, Australia

ISBN 0-87129-207-6

AUTHOR'S NOTES

THE FIFTH SUN presents the life of Oscar Arnulfo Romero from the time of his installation as Archbishop of San Salvador (February 22, 1977) to the day of his assassination (March 24, 1980). It is a dramatic portrait of a human being struggling to cure the ills destroying his people. Rarely does it happen that a person becomes a true hero in the ancient and proper sense of that word, a person who suffers for the well-being of a people. Oscar Romero is one of those few, and that is why I wanted to tell his story.

In the spirit of original tragedy, *THE FIFTH SUN* is a tomb/ritual play that presents the suffering of the hero for the contemplation of the community. It is synthetically constructed, employing elements of Meso-American (Mayan/Nahuatlan) temple dramas, European medieval mystery plays, and tomb rituals of the ancient Near East.

The title comes from the Mayan/Nahuatlan story of the fifth sun, the son of the Lord of the Universe who voluntarily sacrifices himself for the well-being of all creation. Through this sacrifice Nanautzin becomes the fifth sun, the sun that gives light and life to our present world. The Franciscan missionaries, exploiting the obvious analogy here, identified Jesus as the fifth sun, thus facilitating the symbiotic absorption of Catholic myth and ritual into Indian culture. To this day, each religion lives through the other.

Although *THE FIFTH SUN* is based on real events and real people, it is a work of poetic fiction. Every character and every event has been dramatically constructed to reveal Romero and his predicament as I, the playwright, understand them. All the words of this play are my own, except for those of Romero's last sermon which is constructed from his sermon of March 23, 1980 and for those of the congressional hearing which is constructed from several interviews he gave shortly before his assassination.

To My Grandparents

THE FIFTH SUN

A Play in Two Acts
For a flexible cast of 10 to 14 players*

CHARACTERS

OSCAR ROMERO . . . . Archbishop of San Salvador
ANNE DUNN . . . . a Mercy sister from the USA
HECTOR NAVAREZ . . . . a Diocesan priest of San Salvador
RUTILIO GRANDE . . . . a Jesuit priest from El Salvador
THE NUNCIO . . . . papal ambassador to Central America
THE COLONEL . . an officer in the El Salvadoran special forces
KUKULCAN . . . . the Chief Priest and the Lord of Life
AHPUCH . . . . the Lord of Death
CHAC . . . . the Lord of Rain
GHANAN . . . . the Lord of Cultivation

SETTING: El Salvador.
TIME: February 22, 1977 to March 24, 1980.

*The actors playing the Guardian Deities may be male or female. The Guardians, because they embody the spirit and voice of the El Salvadoran people, may also play the villagers, the strike organizers and other roles at the director's discretion. For economy, the size of the cast may be reduced to eight actors with the use of doubling (see Production Notes). In response to many requests, two special versions of *THE FIFTH SUN* have been written to accommodate those groups who wish to employ larger casts and those groups, mostly high school drama classes, who wish to perform a shorter version. The large cast ensemble version of *THE FIFTH SUN* more fully realizes the choral and ritual character of the play. The shorter one-hour version intensifies the dramatic focus of the play on the transformation of Oscar Romero. Both of these special versions are available in typescript form from the publisher.

The professional premiere performance of *THE FIFTH SUN* was given at the Victory Gardens Theater, Chicago, Illinois on September 26 - November 4, 1984, with the following cast:

Oscar Romero .... Jack McLaughlin-Gray
Anne Dunn .... Lorna Raver Johnson
Hector Navarez .... Ray Rodriguez
Rutilio Grande/Assassin .... Ramiro Carrillo
Kukulcan/Nuncio .... William J. Norris
Ahpuch .... Colette Kilroy
Chac .... Jill Holden
Ghanan/Colonel .... Dennis Cockrum

Directed by Dennis Zacek
Set Design by Rick Paul
Costume Design by Patricia Hart
Sound Design by Galen G. Ramsey
Lighting Design by Rita Pietraszek

The writing of this revised version of *THE FIFTH SUN* was provoked by the insights the author gained from his participation in many of the play's productions. He is especially grateful to Juan Ramirez, Artistic Director of Latino Chicago, to Judith Royer, Professor of Drama at Loyola-Marymount University in Los Angeles, and to Iverson Warinner, Professor of Drama at Spalding University in Louisville, Kentucky, for their inspiring production concepts.

ACT ONE

THE FIRST HUNDRED DAYS

SCENE ONE: The Selection/Consecration

(1)

The GUARDIANS speak from their respective compass points (of the theater or of the stage): CHAC, from the south, GHANAN, from the east, AHPUCH from the north, and KUKULCAN from the west.

CHAC.

Where there was neither heaven nor earth
The Word declared itself.

GHANAN.

The Word unfolded itself, all beauty and grace.
And all the vastness of eternity shuddered.

AHPUCH.

And the Word asked its children:
Which one of you will light this world
and give it life, for now it stands
In cold and darkness.

KUKULCAN.

And all were afraid.
For each knew the price.

AHPUCH.

The Word asked again:
Which one of you will give light to the world?
Which one of you will give the world the gift of life?

(The ceremonial drums beat. Then the chanting of DEMONSTRATORS is heard.)

(2)

(ROMERO enters alone. He has just been installed as the new Archbishop of San Salvador by the Apostolic Nuncio. He is still partially attired in the vestments from this ceremony. He hears the chanting of the demonstrators in the street protesting the Government's handling of the recent election. He goes to the window, looks out upon them, starts to pray. Enter the NUNCIO in regular attire. Throughout this subscene the chanting of the DEMONSTRATORS presses upon ROMERO.)

NUNCIO *(responding to the demonstrators chanting and ROMERO's praying)*. Those people never tire of their parades. *(Joins ROMERO at the window.)* We'll never get to lunch on time.

ROMERO. There is considerable evidence that the government tampered with the results of the election.

NUNCIO. My dear Oscar, if they had power there wouldn't be any elections. These revolutionaries think themselves pure and virtuous. They don't know themselves. That's the difference between them and us. *(Pause.)* These are sad times, Oscar. All order has collapsed. How did you put it? So eloquent: "We must keep to the center, hold to the traditional way...Our mission is eminently religious and transcendent..."

ROMERO. While seeking justice...I said while seeking justice.

NUNCIO *(ignoring ROMERO)*. "Our duty," you said, "is to serve our priests and the duty of our priests is to serve the religious needs of the people, not politics." *(While the NUNCIO speaks, ROMERO takes out a small vial which contains a liquid medicine for his stomach. He takes some of the medicine.)* You have a way with words. *(The NUNCIO notices ROMERO taking the medicine.)* Even those who think you without stomach for the job admit that. It's getting late, Oscar, it wouldn't look right to keep President Molina waiting.

ROMERO. Please give the president my apologies.

NUNCIO. A missed lunch is a missed opportunity, and, it can be misconstrued.

ROMERO. I'll send him a personal note.

NUNCIO. Oscar, an illness, even a real illness has political implications. In El Salvador, you are the Church, and that means the Church won't be sitting next to the president at lunch.

ROMERO. I'm sure you'll see to it that everyone properly interprets my absence.

NUNCIO. When the Holy Father asked me who should be archbishop, I chose you.

ROMERO. Yes, I know. Thank you.

NUNCIO. It isn't your thanks that I want. *(Beat.)* Take a little holiday, Oscar. Take a rest, build up your strength. *(The chanting intrudes.)* I'm going to the shore myself. Too noisy here. Disturbs the disgestion.

ROMERO. I was planning to leave tomorrow for Santa Maria, to make my retreat.

NUNCIO. Excellent. Don't worry about things here. *(The chanting gets louder.)* These parades won't last forever. *(The NUNCIO starts to exit. Stops.)* When you get back, I insist you see my personal physician. We must fix this stomach of yours. *(The NUNCIO exits. The chanting of the DEMONSTRATORS nags at ROMERO's conscience, pulls him to the window. He contemplates what is happening on the street. Suddenly gunfire is heard. There are sounds of people screaming and running in panic. ROMERO flees.)*

(3)

OFFSTAGE VOICES.

- Where is Romero?
- Where is the Monsenor?
- We are dying!
- Where is Romero?
- Where is the Archbishop!?

(In the commotion ANNE and HECTOR enter. They run into each other. They are fleeing the National Guard.)

ANNE. Hector, thank God, you're okay.

HECTOR. Where's Romero.

ANNE. In Santa Maria…on retreat.

HECTOR. The bastard! I told you he's one of them. This was planned!

ANNE. We've got to stop this. See if you can get through to Monsenor Chavez. Perhaps he can do something. I'll try to get through to the American ambassador.

(The gunshots get closer and louder. They BOTH flee. The GUARDIANS present themselves.)

AHPUCH. Ahpuch, Lord of Death.

GHANAN. Ghanan, Lord of Corn.

CHAC. Chac, Lord of Rain.

KUKULCAN *(center stage and forward)*. Kukulcan, Lord of Life.

CHAC. To us was entrusted the creation.

ALL. We are the guardians!

GHANAN. To us was entrusted the care of the peoples of this land:

AHPUCH. Of Chiapas

GHANAN. Of the Yucatan

CHAC. Of Guatemala

GHANAN. Of Honduras

AHPUCH. Of El Salvador.

ALL. We are the Bacab Balam! We are the Jaguar Priests of the Sun! *(KUKULCAN places his great shield at the apex of what will become the sun/cross tomb monument for ROMERO.)*

AHPUCH. To us was entrusted the sacrifice!

KUKULCAN. Then and forever!

SCENE TWO: The Call To Service

ANNE and HECTOR in the chancery. One week later.

ANNE. Give me a cigarette.

HECTOR. Why, Sister Anne, I thought you quit smoking for Lent.

ANNE. I need the butt-ends to kill the aphids on my begonias.

HECTOR. Women are not supposed to smoke in front of archbishops.

ANNE. If an archbishop doesn't want me to smoke, he shouldn't summon me to the chancery and keep me waiting for an hour. *(HECTOR gives her a cigarette. She lights it herself.)*

HECTOR. Come the revolution...

ANNE. I know...there will be no aphids on my begonias.

HECTOR. No. They have to live too. Come the revolution we shall summon the Archbishop to explain himself to us and we'll keep him waiting for two hours.

ANNE. God! I hate waiting, especially to be told I've been naughty and have to be sent home...especially when I've already decided to go home.

HECTOR. Quit before you're fired. Saves face. Did they teach you that at the University of Chicago?

ANNE. Unfortunately, I've been educated for success only. First my father, then my teachers. No one ever taught me anything about failure.

(RUTILIO enters.)

RUTILIO. My God, *(Greeting in Spanish to HECTOR.)* it's good to see you. *(RUTILIO embraces them both.)* I heard you were both trapped in Rosario Church.

ANNE. We were lucky.

HECTOR. Anne's good looks got us through the (National) Guard lines.

RUTILIO. Thank God you're okay. How many died?

ANNE. Anywhere between eighty and three hundred. It's hard to tell. We're conducting a canvass.

HECTOR. Our new Archbishop was conveniently out of town.

RUTILIO. He was on retreat.

HECTOR. It was planned.

ANNE. Since he took office, the government has expelled six priests and four nuns.

RUTILIO. I'm sure he had nothing to do with that.

ANNE. He didn't stop it.

RUTILIO. He was trained as a spiritual director, not a politician. Give him a chance.

HECTOR. We don't have time for on-the-job training. People are dying. Don't let your friendship with him cloud your vision.

ANNE. We need a leader, now.

HECTOR. He's a weak old woman. *(Repeats in Spanish to RUTILIO.)* That's why they picked him. They're going to use him to destroy us.

ANNE. One more weak old woman out of you, Hector, and I'm going to abandon a lifetime of nonviolence.

RUTILIO. Don't prejudge him. He's a good man.

HECTOR. We don't need a saint. We need a prince. Someone who knows power and how to use it.

(Enter ROMERO. Those who are seated rise.)

ROMERO. Sorry to keep you waiting. *(He embraces RUTILIO.)* Good to see you, my friend. Please be seated. I have called you here to discuss your work with the grassroots communities. Some of your communities have been conducting Eucharistic services without a priest...

ANNE. Monsenor, if they waited for a priest, they could only have mass twice a year.

ROMERO. Lay people must not usurp the role of the priest.

RUTILIO. These are extreme situations, Monsenor, extreme times. The people are not attacking the authority of the Church. They are meeting their needs for the sacraments.

ROMERO. Your Jesuit seminarians, Rutilio, are organizing the campesinos of Aguilares into labor unions. That's politics, not religion.

HECTOR. Justice is the work of every Christian.

ROMERO. And you, Fr. Navarez, have been leading workers on strikes, teaching them Marxist economics.

HECTOR. Before we talk about us, I want to talk about you. I want to know why you were so conspicuously absent when the National Guard was murdering our people in Plaza Libertad.

ROMERO *(visibly disturbed)*. Church law requires that I make a retreat before I assume the responsibilities of my office.

HECTOR. How convenient for the government death squads.

ROMERO. I needed to prepare myself.

HECTOR. Those who plunder the people are always ready. They don't need to go on retreats to prepare themselves. You went to Santa Maria because you knew they were planning to attack us. Whose side are you on?!

ROMERO. I'm on no one's side! *(Takes medicine.)* I am pastor to all the people.

HECTOR. I know that's what they taught you to say in Rome, but this is the real world. Here, in El Salvador, you are on the side of the poor or you're on the side of the Oligarchy.

ROMERO. In the real world, Hector, taking sides leads to death. The only place taking sides accomplishes anything is in your ideological fantasies. There is no necessary antagonism between the rich and the poor. The rich are called to service.

HECTOR. They are wolves!

ROMERO. The rich are called to use their wealth and position for the welfare of the whole community.

ANNE. The Fourteen Families take the wealth of this nation and put it into Swiss bank accounts.

RUTILIO. Monsenor, there are those who say you were made Archbishop to destroy us.

ROMERO. The government sees your communities as communist cells. My brother bishops see your communities as threats to—

ANNE *(interrupting)*. What do you see us as?

(As ROMERO contemplates his answer, the GUARDIANS appear and slowly surround him. They are voices of his conscience, reminding him of the Gospel. He speaks to them as if they were Jesus and he were Peter.)

KUKULCAN. Simon Peter, why are you troubled?

AHPUCH. Are they casting out devils in my name?

ROMERO. Yes, Lord.

GHANAN. Are they curing the sick in my name?

ROMERO. Yes, Lord.

CHAC. Are they preaching the Gospel to the poor?

ROMERO. Yes, Lord.

ALL. Are these not the signs of the kingdom? Are these not the signs of the reign of God?

KUKULCAN. Then, why are you troubled? *(ROMERO returns to ordinary time and space.)*

ROMERO. I need more time...I will visit every family who lost someone in the massacre in Plaza Libertad. We will have a public funeral mass—

HECTOR *(interrupting)*. We don't need prayers.

RUTILIO. Monsenor, my people need your support. The plantation owners keep taking more and more of their land.

ROMERO. We shall protect their lands in the courts.

ANNE. We have cases pending in the courts since 1970.

HECTOR. Elementary politics: The landowners own the judges.

ROMERO. I will speak personally to President Molina.

HECTOR. That will accomplish nothing and you know it.

ROMERO *(angry)*. What would you have me do? Because of your work, already one factory owner has been killed, three factories bombed! Violence breeds violence. Jesus told Peter to sheath his sword. He said: Those who live by the sword shall die by it. We are supposed to be peacemakers.

HECTOR. St. Thomas says a person has a right to defend his liberty with force if necessary.

ROMERO. I will never support violence!

RUTILIO. Monsenor, the United States government is building a road to Aguilares...*(As RUTILIO speaks, the GUARDIANS begin to chant softly.)*

GUARDIANS.

First the Road, then the Soldiers
First the Road, then no Land

RUTILIO. ...once the road is built, the large landowners will extend their cotton plantations. My people will be forced off their land. They'll be forced to move to the city or to work on the plantations. They won't be able to grow food anymore to feed themselves...

(The chanting of the GUARDIANS builds. The GUARDIANS become visible and encircle ROMERO as the narration develops.)

ROMERO. I will speak to the American Ambassador.

RUTILIO. Fourteen villagers have died already.

ROMERO. I will speak to President Molina.

RUTILIO. My people can't eat cotton!

ROMERO. We must educate all sides. Violence is not the answer. Jesus stood naked before his accusers. Before the entire might of Rome and Jerusalem he stood naked. We follow him, not Karl Marx, not even Thomas Aquinas. We are priests and nuns of Jesus Christ. We are dedicated to the Gospel, to the conversion of all peoples, to the reconciliation of all classes, rich and poor. You don't do that with a gun!

HECTOR. With a prayer, I suppose. *(AHPUCH hands ROMERO a note.)*

ROMERO. There's been some trouble in Aguilares...paratroopers.

ANNE. Oh my God!

HECTOR. The bastards! *(RUTILIO exits.)*

ROMERO. Rutilio, I'll go with you. *(Exit ROMERO.)*

SCENE THREE: Hearing The Call

The GUARDIANS playing the people of Aguilares chant and dance a maize ritual.

THE MAIZE PRAYER AND RITUAL*

VILLAGERS.

- Oh Holy God
- Our Grandfather, Our Grandmother
- God of the mountains
- God of the valleys
- God of all the earth
- Be gracious
- Be patient
- Bless our work
- It is needful

** Author's rendition of an authentic prayer of the Indians of El Salvador.*

- It is necessary for our life
- Bless what we sow here
- Bless this *milpa*
- Guard it for us
- Guard it from this time of sowing
- Till the time of the harvest
- For us
- For our children

- From the Great Lord Kukulcan, the Sacred Red Kernel
- From the Great Lord Ghanan, the Rites of Cultivation
- From the Great Lord Chac, the Life-Giving Rains
- From Generation to Generation

(As the ritual comes to a close, the sound of helicopters begins to be heard. This sound steadily increases into a terrifying, deafening din. The chant from the previous scene is heard.)

- First the Road, then the Soldiers
- First the Road, then no Land

(The helicopter gunships fire down on them. They scatter, they fall, they die, screaming.)

- No Land. No Corn. No Land. No Food.
- The Blood of our Children Soaks the Earth!

(An unholy silence. Enter ROMERO and RUTILIO. The GUARDIANS rise from the Earth, encircle ROMERO, press him.)

GUARDIANS.

- From the heavens they fired upon us
- Like vultures they fell on us from the sky
- They killed my father
- What will you do, Romero?

- They killed my mother
- What will you do, Romero?
- They killed my sister
- They killed my brother
- What will you do, Romero? What will you do?

(KUKULCAN hands a megaphone to a dazed ROMERO. ROMERO tries to address the VILLAGERS.)

ROMERO. My brothers and sisters, I have come to share your grief. I have come to weep with you. I have come to pray with you…

VILLAGERS.

No more words
No more tears
What will you do, Romero?
What will you do?

ROMERO. My brothers and sisters, Christ promises us—

VILLAGERS.

No more words
No more tears
No more prayers

(The VILLAGERS tear the megaphone from ROMERO's hands. This act injures his forehead, causing some slight bleeding. The VILLAGERS press ROMERO with their chant. RUTILIO intercedes, guides ROMERO to a safe spot. The VILLAGERS continue with their rally.)

RUTILIO. They didn't mean to hurt you.

ROMERO. I'm all right. How many were killed?

RUTILIO. Fifty...the paratroopers just went berserk and started killing people.

ROMERO. Why wouldn't they let me speak? I came to mourn with them, to comfort them...

RUTILIO. They didn't mean to hurt you, Monsenor. They want to know what you're going to do.

ROMERO. I'm doing it! I'm their pastor. This is what I'm supposed to be doing. I've come all the way from San Salvador to be with them. I've walked miles in the hot sun without food or water. When was the last time their bishop came to minister to them?

RUTILIO. You are the first.

ROMERO. I've come to pray with them, to offer them the consolation of the sacraments. That's my duty.

RUTILIO. They mean no disrespect. Their faith is very strong.

ROMERO. I need some water. I need something to eat.

RUTILIO. The paratroopers fouled the well and burned the granary.

ROMERO. I need something to settle my stomach. In all the commotion I forgot my medicine. *(While RUTILIO asks the VILLAGERS for food, ROMERO looks for a place to rest.)*

RUTILIO. They say there is nothing, but they will look.

ROMERO. Rutilio, I can't do this. I'm not prepared.

RUTILIO. No one is.

ROMERO. You know what I was doing on my retreat while the people were being massacred in Plaza Libertad? I was preparing a talk on the Spiritual Formation of diocesan priests. I have it here with me. *(Takes some notes out of his cassock.)* I've spent my whole life studying spirituality. I'm not a politician. I'm not a leader. I can't do this.

RUTILIO. God chose you.

ROMERO. I'm weak, Rutilio. I need my hot bath in the morning. I need my siesta in the afternoon. And I'm afraid.

RUTILIO. God is a good Marxist, Monsenor. He takes from each according to his capacity and gives to each according to his need.

(Enter CHAC AS A YOUNG GIRL. She gives ROMERO an old tortilla and a Coca-Cola. ROMERO takes the food, starts to eat.)

ROMERO. Thank you, little sister. Would you like some? *(The CHILD shakes her head no. To RUTILIO.)* Of course, the ubiquitous Coca-Cola. Thanks to American ingenuity: no water, but plenty of Coke. *(To the CHILD.)* Thank your mother for me, little one.

CHAC AS A YOUNG GIRL. My mother is dead.

ROMERO. I'm sorry, my daughter. I'm sorry.

CHAC AS A YOUNG GIRL. My father is dead.

ROMERO. Have you no one?

CHAC AS A YOUNG GIRL. I was saving this tortilla for my brother. Now he is dead.

(ROMERO reaches out to embrace her. The CHILD pushes him away, transforms herself into CHAC, screams.)

CHAC. What will you do, Romero? What will you do!? *(Blackout.)*

SCENE FOUR: The Gesture

A few days later. ANNE is in the chancery. She is sorting through some papers. Enter HECTOR.

HECTOR. Well, I see you're still on the job.

ANNE. I'm just tidying up some things. I hate loose ends. Are you here on official business or just snooping?

HECTOR. I got an urgent, secret message by carrier iguana… something about our radio station.

ANNE. Oh no! It's not been bombed again!?

HECTOR. Something about a new hook-up, very top-secret.

ANNE. Well, I don't send messages by iguana. So you're in the wrong office.

HECTOR. I'm sure you've heard about those two Americans they assassinated last night at the Sheraton?

ANNE. Yes, I heard.

HECTOR. So, tell me. Why did the CIA have our colonels kill your agents?

ANNE. They weren't agents.

HECTOR. Everyone who works for the American Institute for Free Labor is a CIA agent.

ANNE. I wasn't.

HECTOR. The exception that proves the rules.

ANNE. Does your Marxist metaphysics absolutely preclude the possibility of anyone acting altruistically for the good of others?

HECTOR. Yes.

ANNE. So then, you have the same cynical view of human nature as capitalism. Self interst; class interest: greed, greed, greed.

HECTOR. My view is realistic…

ANNE. Cynical.

HECTOR. …and unlike capitalism, Marxism seeks to change human nature, for the better.

ANNE. That makes you naive and dangerous, as well as cynical.

HECTOR. Those are strong words for an alien do-gooder trying to save us retarded third world types.

ANNE. I'll admit to the alien part.

HECTOR. You're not your average do-gooder. More complex, more sophisticated, but, nonetheless, a do-gooder.

ANNE. And what are you? I mean apart from all this Marxist rhetoric.

HECTOR. Me? Why shucks, ma'am, I'm just a radio repair man, just doing my job. *(Beat.)* Speaking of naive and dangerous, I saw that article you wrote for your sisters in the States, what do you call that thing?

ANNE. The Justice and Peace Network.

HECTOR. Yes, that. It was a piece of shit.

ANNE. Thank you very much.

HECTOR. A classic example of degenerate liberal sentimentality.

ANNE. Hector, my article might be a piece of shit, but it is not liberal.

HECTOR. What do you know about Indians?

ANNE. Not very much.

HECTOR. Then you shouldn't write about them.

ANNE. They fascinate me.

HECTOR. Go to Guatemala where they haven't killed us all, yet. There, at least, we still have a semblance of our own culture.

ANNE. I didn't know you were Indian.

HECTOR. You didn't recognize my noble savage manner. Since La Matanza, we've learned how to pass...is that how you say it?

ANNE. Your command of American English has always amazed and intimidated me. I'm sorry if my article offended you.

HECTOR. No need to apologize. It's not the first, nor is it the worst piece of shit I've read about Indians by alien do-gooders.

(Enter ROMERO.)

ROMERO. Hector, I'm glad you're here. I have a job for you. I want you to install a hook-up here to our radio station. I want people to be able to come here and voice their opinions over the radio in the safety of the chancery. You might have to knock a few walls down.

HECTOR. Even those of your private office?

ROMERO. If necessary.

HECTOR. How will you make all those secret deals with the colonels?

ROMERO. I'll keep the key to my private toilet. Please see to it right away.

HECTOR. Yes, Your Eminence. *(Exit HECTOR.)*

ANNE. Oh, I almost forgot. The Nuncio phoned.

ROMERO. Did you tell him I was out with my girl friends? All twenty-seven of them?

ANNE. As a matter of fact I did.

ROMERO. Anne, if anyone can get me through this ordeal, it will be those nuns with whom I live and pray.

ANNE. I'm sure they're wonderful women.

ROMERO. Ah, the terrifying condescension of the young!

ANNE. I'm not that young. And I didn't mean to be condescending.

ROMERO. I know you American nuns like to be more involved in the world than my Carmelites, or myself, for that matter...

ANNE. I think that prayer and fasting have their place in the scheme of things, but I also think an archbishop could use more worldly advisors.

ROMERO. Like yourself.

ANNE. I wasn't suggesting that.

ROMERO. What were you suggesting?

ANNE. You need to have the best information, the best data available when you face the American Ambassador or the Vatican. You need to have a complete understanding of the economic situation in this country. That's the only way you'll get anywhere.

ROMERO. All right. So I need somebody who understands the workings of the International Monetary Fund, the procedures of the World Bank, the U.S. economic system, and the economic infrastructure of El Salvador. Right?

ANNE *(impressed)*. Right.

ROMERO. Good. I'm glad you agree with me. Therefore, I do not accept your pro-forma resignation and re-appoint you to the Archdiocesan staff as our chief advisor on economics. I promise only to listen to what you have to say, not to obey you. And I will never change my mind about women being priests. But you don't have to make the coffee. I make it so much better than you do.

ANNE. Monsenor, don't you think…

ROMERO. There's no need to thank me. You may go now.

SCENE FIVE: The Way To His Heart

ROMERO moves from the chancery to the village of Aguilares. A GUARDIAN gives ROMERO a carpenter's bag. As ROMERO moves to the village, we see RUTILIO busy helping with the repairs in his village. The GUARDIANS chant and dance a sacrifice ritual that indicates that the sacrificial death of RUTILIO is the key to opening ROMERO's heart to his sacred duty and destiny.

GUARDIANS.

He must be spotless
He must be loved
Pure
Without Blemish
The Perfect Sacrifice
Prepare the Altar
Sound the Drum
Life for Life
Blood for Blood
He must be loved

(ROMERO joins RUTILIO in the work; he is repairing a damaged tabernacle canopy.)

ROMERO. I love the air here. It reminds me of Barrios when I was a boy. It's good to see the people busy repairing their homes.

RUTILIO. Thanks to you. I know how poor the diocesan treasury is.

ROMERO. I'll have to learn to eat more beans and less meat. *(He pats his stomach.)* It'll do my stomach good.

RUTILIO. I tried to refinish the canopy over the tabernacle like you showed me. I'm afraid I don't have your master's touch. When you get tired of being Archbishop, you can open up a carpenter's shop here in Aguilares. You've become quite popular, you know.

ROMERO. You mean your parishioners no longer want to punch me in the nose *(no quieren romperme la cara)*?

RUTILIO. Well, maybe one or two. Why don't you stay with us till Sunday for the Fiesta?

ROMERO. I have the devil to pay as it is for this brief time I've stolen. You shouldn't tempt me, Rutilio. If you're not careful, I'll appoint myself pastor here, and make you go and deal with the Nuncio and my brother bishops.

RUTILIO. Monsenor, I thought you were my friend!

ROMERO. All's fair in love and war. I'll help you with that canopy before I leave this afternoon.

RUTILIO. At least stay for our community meeting tonight.

ROMERO. Rutilio, I'm worried. Some colonel from the Ministry of Defense paid me a visit last night.

RUTILIO. To tell you what a fine job you're doing no doubt.

ROMERO. There is evidence to suggest that Hector is a member of the FPL.

RUTILIO. Evidence is easily manufactured.

ROMERO. Is he?

RUTILIO. Monsenor, I have chosen never to touch a gun. But I can understand why a brother priest might choose otherwise. *(ROMERO tries to interrupt, RUTILIO gestures for him to listen.)* In the mountains once, I got lost. I came upon this large hut. There were six coffins in it. They were simple coffins like we use all the time, except they each had this little hole in the lid with a drinking straw in it. There was this terrible odor. Then I heard this sound. It seemed to come from one of the coffins. I went over. The stench made me very sick. I heard this sound again. I tried to open the lid. It was nailed down very tight. I got some tools from my jeep. *(The pain of the memory overwhelms RUTILIO. He recovers himself.)* Inside each coffin was a living corpse, a living dead man. Those thugs from Orden had kept them alive, to torture them. They fed them a little *atole* everyday just to torture them. I went to get some help. There was nothing we could do. Their bodies...We had to let them die. *(Beat.)* Monsenor, I wanted to kill those bastards from Orden! I wanted to kill them. And I wanted to kill those poor people in the coffins, to put them out of their misery. And I wanted to kill myself too. *(Beat.)* Sometimes my doubts are stronger than my faith.

ROMERO. It is never wrong to forgive. We must forgive them and ourselves.

RUTILIO. Monsenor, I'm as old-fashioned as you are. I still say the rosary before I go to bed. But, there are priests who have taken up the gun. I do not agree with them, but I do not judge them.

ROMERO *(beat)*. I must. *(Beat.)* Have you ever heard of the White Warriors of Christ?

RUTILIO. No. And I'm sure I don't care to. I don't need to hear about another gang of murderers.

ROMERO. According to this colonel, this organization has drawn up a list of priests…I've seen it.

RUTILIO. A death list.

ROMERO. I warned him, Rutilio. I told him to tell those White Warriors: My priests are sacred to me. They are my sons. I alone command them. I alone correct them. They shall not touch a hair of your head.

GUARDIANS *(chanting and dancing)*.

The way to his heart
Now is the time
Strike quick
Strike deep
He is spotless
He is loved
Prepare the altar
Prepare the offering
Blood for blood
Life for life
The way to his heart is open

(As the GUARDIANS chant and dance, ROMERO and RUTILIO slowly fade out. The lighting shifts to the chancery.)

SCENE SIX: Piercing His Heart

March 12, 1977. ANNE is in the chancery talking long distance on the phone. She chain-smokes.

ANNE. It was terrible. It's hard to describe. I've tried to write some things. We're still canvassing to see how many died or "disappeared." Now the National Guard's attacking the mountain villages. It's not like when we were in Mississippi. It's not like the west side of Chicago. It's not like anything...Mary! Damn connection! Three days for this damn call to get through. Oh, good. Just tell me real quick before we get cut off again. How are Elizabeth and Sara? Have you heard anything from Angela and Eddy?... A girl! Wonderful!...Oh, a boy. Well, that's wonderful too. I'm having trouble hearing you...Yes, Betty got through okay. And all the peanut butter too. She crossed the border from Guatemala...Great! When?...Look, I know this is decadent as hell, but I'd kill for a bottle of pH balanced shampoo.

(ROMERO enters unnoticed.)

ANNE. Tell Debbie to bring the real fancy kind. She has the socialist tendency to get inferior products... I don't know. He's not easy to figure out. I don't know what he's going to do. I really don't feel comfortable...Mary, Mary! Damn it! *(ANNE clicks the switch, speaks to the operator in Spanish, slams the phone down.)* Can't they do anything right in this country!?

ROMERO. We make good lovers, so I'm told.

ANNE *(very embarrassed, attempts to hide her cigarettes).* I'm sorry. My Irish temper. And my North American arrogance.

ROMERO. You don't need to hide your cigarettes from me. I know you smoke.

ANNE. I've been told by an impeccable authority that women are not supposed to smoke in front of archbishops.

ROMERO. In front of any man.

ANNE. I'm a compromiser, Monsenor. So until we have women archbishops I won't smoke in front of one. As for the rest of the men of El Salvador, they'll have to deal with it.

ROMERO. I'm thinking to write your President Carter as you suggest.

ANNE. He seems serious about human rights.

ROMERO *(pensively).* I believe that, but can he understand what's happening in El Salvador?! *(Beat.)* The air is so heavy. I can hardly breathe.

ANNE. The rains are late.

ROMERO. Don't you miss your family?

ANNE. My mother's dead. I have no brothers and sisters. And my father and I are too much alike.

ROMERO. He didn't want you to be a nun.

ANNE. President of First National Bank.

ROMERO. You could have.

ANNE. You overrate me and underrate sexism in Chicago.

ROMERO. My father wanted me to be a carpenter. It's hard to go against the wishes of your family. *(Beat.)* I wish it would rain.

ANNE. March is a lousy month. My father always used to say that no one should ever make a decision in March. But my mother said that March was the best time to make decisions because it was the only time you felt rotten enough to change things.

ROMERO. I think your mother and I may be kindred souls.

(As ROMERO speaks this last line, lights go up on another section of the stage, on RUTILIO and MANUEL [played by a GUARDIAN] who are preparing to go to El Paisnal to say mass. The focus shifts from the chancery to Aguilares and back.)

(At AGUILARES.)

RUTILIO. Is everything ready?

MANUEL. Yes, Father.

RUTILIO. You always forget the oils for anointing the sick.

MANUEL. I've packed them, Father.

(The CHANCERY.)

ROMERO. Perhaps March is so grim so that the joy of Easter will be that much more exultant. You should phone your father, Anne. You should tell him you love him.

ANNE. I wish it would rain.

(At AGUILARES.)

MANUEL. Father, can we stop by my sister's on our way. I told her I would bring her some yarn.

RUTILIO. We don't have time, Manuel. You know how your sister is. She'll make us stay to have some *atole* and tell us in great detail every pain she has had since our last visit.

MANUEL. I swear, Father, we won't even get out of the jeep.

RUTILIO. See if Nelson is ready. We must get going. *(Hurries MANUEL in Spanish. As RUTILIO speaks these last words, he and MANUEL are gunned down by machine gun fire.)*

ROMERO *(screaming)*. No! No! No!

(The VOICE OF HECTOR is heard speaking wildly over the chancery's radio hookup. CHAC enters and hangs his great shield on the tomb monument while HECTOR speaks.)

HECTOR'S VOICE. People of El Salvador! Wake Up! Wake Up! They have murdered our brother. On the 12th of March, 1977, they have murdered our brother Fr. Rutilio Grande because he loved the poor. They will tell lies. They will tell you he was a terrorist, a communist, that he had mistresses. They will do anything to discredit him because the truth is that he was a true Christian, a true saint. They killed him because he loved us…

SCENE SEVEN: The Resolve

(1)

ROMERO and the NUNCIO in the chancery.

NUNCIO. You cannot do it.

ROMERO. I am the Archbishop.

NUNCIO. It is illegal.

ROMERO. My staff has thoroughly researched the matter. I have the right.

NUNCIO. What staff? You mean that foreign nun, that communist from America?

ROMERO. She studied at the University of Chicago, under Milton Friedman. I don't think Dr. Friedman's a communist.

NUNCIO. I forbid it. As your superior, I forbid it.

ROMERO. Your Excellency, I want always to obey you when I can. But I am the Archbishop of San Salvador. In my diocese, I represent the authority of the Apostles and of Jesus Christ. *(Beat.)* My priests support me. They voted eighty-two to one to support my actions.

NUNCIO. The Church is not a democracy. *(Beat.)* They've got a ring through your nose, those foreign nuns! They lead you around like a gelded bull. You even let them teach communism in the schools.

ROMERO. They teach social justice.

NUNCIO. Marxism!

ROMERO. I personally approved the texts they are using. All the teaching materials are based on the social teachings of papal encyclicals.

NUNCIO. Oscar, everywhere the Marxists have gained power they have sought to control the Church, they have suppressed the religion of the people, and they have violated basic human rights. Don't play into their hands.

ROMERO. I am not a politician. I am not supporting Marxists or anyone else. I am only trying to follow the Gospel and the teachings of the Church.

NUNCIO. The Marxists will exploit your actions. They will use you to deceive the people. Then when they have power they will destroy you. The death of Rutilio is a heinous act, a tragedy, but it is nothing compared to a communist takeover of El Salvador. I have advised the Pope to remove all foreign missionaries from El Salvador.

ROMERO. That would leave me with a mere handful of priests and nuns.

NUNCIO. The American nuns will go first. Then the Jesuits.

ROMERO. You are a foreigner, and that priest you so generously assigned to my staff to spy on me.

NUNCIO. Oscar, you are letting your passions get the best of you. I like you. I hope to see you in Rome, a cardinal. Fr. Grande was playing politics, the wrong kind of politics.

ROMERO. He was teaching campesinos to read and write.

NUNCIO. He was organizing peasants into labor collectives. That is illegal in El Salvador.

ROMERO. Since Leo XIII the Church has affirmed the right of workers to form unions.

NUNCIO. He was attacking the institution of private property. Stop playing the *ingénue* with me! What you are planning to do is an act of war. You're letting your Creole blood cloud your judgment! You are declaring war on this government! You are a politician. You are playing politics. And you're not very good at it. I will not support you. Rome will not support you.

ROMERO. You all have your ideas of who I am, of what I am supposed to do, of what I am supposed to say. Where is God in all of this? Does no one consider the simple right and wrong of things!

NUNCIO. You are either playing the fool, or you are a fool! *(NUNCIO fades away.)*

(2)

(The COLONEL becomes visible.)

ROMERO. I told you not to touch my priests.

COLONEL. I gave you fair warning. If you do this thing, Rutilio will be but the first of many.

ROMERO. They won't let you.

COLONEL. Let me tell you something, Archbishop. The government needs men like me. Washington will support anyone who shouts slogans against the Russians. And the Nuncio? The Nuncio thinks he's playing chess with the Devil. A few priests, a few pawns in the game. *(Takes ROMERO by the arm, leads him to the window.)* Do this thing and watch closely what happens. Watch the blood flow, the governments change, and see who is on top in the end when all the shooting stops.

ROMERO. Colonel, I have no power except the power Christ gave me: to preach his Gospel, to forgive sins, to rebuke evil. Now, it is my duty to rebuke evil.

(The COLONEL fades out. ROMERO moves to the sacristy of the cathedral. ANNE appears.)

ANNE. Are you sure, Monsenor? There is still time. *(While ROMERO gives the following response to ANNE, the GUARDIANS begin to vest ROMERO in the sacred robes of his office in preparation for the excommunication ceremony which will be broadcast throughout all El Salvador over the Archdiocesan Radio Station.)*

ROMERO. Anne, when I was in the seminary in Rome, when I was taking my oral examinations for my licentiate in theology, I was getting very confused and upset. I couldn't get anything right. An old Italian priest was sitting way in the corner. He appeared to be sleeping. His old cassock was full of soup and coffee stains. He opened one eye and asked me this question: "Father, what is the whole of the law? What is our sole purpose for being here, right now?" I couldn't answer. I was too full of theology, and philosophy, and history, and politics. Too full of opinions! The old priest took pity on me. This is what he said to me: "This is all that Jesus taught, this is the whole of the law—Love God with your whole heart, and your whole soul, and your whole mind. And how do you do this? You do this by loving your neighbor as you love yourself." This is the law that Rutilio lived. It is the simple message of Jesus, whether we ride horses, or drive cars, or walk, whether we wear shoes or go barefoot. No one who lives this law will injure himself or his neighbor.

ANNE. When you were made Archbishop, Hector said we needed a prince, not a saint.

ROMERO. Whatever you needed, I am what you got. We can only hope God knows what he's doing. *(ANNE hands ROMERO his crozier, the staff of his office, the symbol of his teaching authority. ROMERO moves to the sanctuary where he addresses the congregation. The GUARDIANS act as his attendants.)* Today, I have sent this letter to President Molina. It is very short: "In the past, the Church has sought to cooperate with you and your government in a common search for the true progress of the people of El Salvador. In the past, we have sought a dialogue with you on the great problems facing the poor. No longer. We will no longer sit at table with you. We will no longer break bread with you. We will no longer talk with you, until you have delivered to the people of El Salvador a full and satisfactory explanation for the murder of Fr. Rutilio Grande and his companions, Nelson and Manuel, and until you have demonstrated a firm resolve to prevent such killings in the future. Until that day we hold you and your government responsible for these heinous acts against the people." *(A GUARDIAN takes ROMERO's crozier. Another GUARDIAN gives him a large candle.)* By the authority given to me by Peter, by the power given to me by Jesus the Christ, I solemnly sever from our sacred body. *(With these words ROMERO breaks a candle, hands the broken pieces to a GUARDIAN. A GUARDIAN hands him a chal-*

ice and a bowl.) I solemnly sever from our sacred blood. *(With these words ROMERO pours some wine into the bowl, hands both chalice and bowl to a GUARDIAN. Another GUARDIAN hands him his crozier. ROMERO bangs the crozier three times on the ground.)* I solemnly excommunicate from the People of God—those who murdered Rutilio, Nelson, and Manuel—*(Bangs his staff three times.)*—those who directly or indirectly ordered them to commit these murders. Three days ago they killed three men. Today we are gathered here 100,000 strong! They have passed a law banning all public gatherings. But there is a law above the law of the State, and that law is the law we follow now. *(Beat.)* Every Sunday I will gather up the cries of the people...

HECTOR and ANNE. Lord, hear our prayers.

ROMERO. Every Sunday I will be the voice of the people, living and dead...

HECTOR and ANNE. Lord, hasten to help us.

ROMERO. Every Sunday I will broadcast the names of those martyred and tortured...

HECTOR and ANNE. Lord, hear our cries. *(The GUARDIANS begin to chant the names of the martyred dead of El Salvador.)*

ROMERO. We follow the Gospel, as Rutilio did...

GUARDIAN. Alfonso Navarro

ROMERO. Presente!

GUARDIAN. Apolinaro Serrano

ROMERO. Presente!

GUARDIAN. Leticia Zamora

ROMERO. Presente!

GUARDIAN. Enrique Alvarez

ROMERO. Presente!

GUARDIAN. Juan Chacon
ROMERO. Presente!
GUARDIAN. Anna Maria Barrera (Serrano)
HECTOR and ANNE. Presente!
ROMERO. Fr. Rutilio Grande of the Society of Jesus.
ALL. Presente!

(When ROMERO speaks the name of RUTILIO the ceremonial drums start their ritual beat. When the GUARDIANS shout their last "Presente" they move into their ritual postures for the ceremony of the Fifth Sun.)

KUKULCAN. In each age the call
AHPUCH. In each age the sacrifice
ALL GUARDIANS. We are the four suns of the cosmos
AHPUCH. Ahpuch, Sun of the North
GHANAN. Ghanan, Sun of the East
CHAC. Chac, Sun of the South
KUKULCAN. Kukulcan, Sun of the West
ALL GUARDIANS.
We are the Bacab Balam. We are the four corners of time and space.

(With this utterance the GUARDIANS form the ceremonial cosmic grid with ROMERO in the center.)

CHAC. Where there was neither heaven nor earth
GHANAN. The Word unfolded itself, all beauty and grace.

KUKULCAN.
And the Word asked his sons:
Which one of you will light this world and give it life
For now it stands in cold and darkness.

AHPUCH.

And none was willing for they knew the price.
And the Word asked again:
Which one of you will give light to the world?
Which one of you will give my creation the gift of life?

GHANAN.

And while the fearful sons debated
Nanautzin whom they deemed too low to consider
Heard his Father's call.

CHAC.

And while the others debated
Nanautzin gathered all his courage
Climbed the steep steps of the great temple
Cast himself into the sacred fire.

AHPUCH.

His frail body cracked and burned.
His pure heart shot forth into the heavens.

ALL GUARDIANS. Unto each age
KUKULCAN. Unto each age is given a guardian
ALL GUARDIANS. Unto each age
KUKULCAN. Unto each age a Sun

ALL GUARDIANS.

In each age the sacrifice
In each age the birth of a New Sun

KUKULCAN. The Fifth Sun
GUARDIANS. The Sun of the Center
AHPUCH. The Sun of the People

ALL GUARDIANS.
To give light!
To give life!

END OF ACT ONE

ACT TWO

THE CONVERSION TO THE POOR

SCENE ONE: The Choice

(1)

The COLONEL is addressing a meeting of the White Warriors. He alone is visible, except for ROMERO who is somewhat visible as if a portrait in the background.

COLONEL. Patriots! A dark cancer gnaws at the heart of our nation! Like a giant octopus its black tentacles creep into every sector of our society. This black beast is eating away the moral fiber of our youth. It seduces them with so-called humanitarian ideas. In the name of human rights and social justice, it perverts their natural idealism for unnatural ends. Contemplate the head of this great octopus. What do you see? Do you see a man? a strong, virile man? a true son of El Salvador! No! You see a drug addict, a homosexual, an internationalist! He has deceived Rome! He has deceived Washington! But he has not deceived us. We, the White Warriors, are not deceived by these false Christians, these castrated men and women in black robes who are making our children soft and effeminate, robbing them of their manhood and of their birthright, making them soft clay to be molded into socialist slaves by their red masters. We must fight this black beast! We are the surgeons of Christ. We must act now to cut out this corruption from our body. We are men! We do not wait for others to tell us what to do! This is our country! These are our children! We are the true sons and fathers of El Salvador! BE A PATRIOT, KILL A PRIEST! BE A PATRIOT, KILL A NUN! Sever the hands and feet of this black monster! Then I shall squash its helpless head under the heels of my boots! *(The light on the COLONEL goes out.)*

(2)

(The light on ROMERO comes on full. Enter ANNE, very excited.)

ANNE. Monsenor, there's been a coup! They're forming a civilian government!

(Enter HECTOR.)

HECTOR. What the hell's going on? The paratroopers have surrounded the presidential palace, the radio stations have gone dead.

ANNE. There's been a coup. I'm working on a statement right now.

HECTOR. What kind of statement?

ANNE. Of support, of course! This will be the first civilian government in fifty years.

HECTOR. Anne, I really thought you had more savvy than this. The generals have no intention of giving up any real power.

ANNE. Both the Christian Democrats and the Communists have agreed to participate.

HECTOR *(to ANNE)*. You're deluding yourself. *(To ROMERO.)* Monsenor, don't support this coup.

ANNE. This is El Salvador's first chance to have a truly democratic government.

HECTOR. The only way to get a truly democratic government is by a revolution of the people, not a coup by the army.

ANNE. That's just ideological bullshit!

ROMERO. We cannot support them.

ANNE. Monsenor, we've dreamt of this moment.

ROMERO. It isn't proper for the Church to support governments or political parties. I cannot say to my priests: "Stay out of politics, stick to the Gospel," if I go around endorsing coups.

ANNE. Your excommunication brought down this government. You cannot pretend you're not involved.

ROMERO. When the government acts unjustly, it is my duty to condemn that injustice.

ANNE. If you don't endorse this government, the people will conclude that you oppose it.

HECTOR. Exactly! And that's why you should not endorse it. You should support the people's struggle to form their own government.

ROMERO. Hector, I don't have the power you think I have. And even if I did, it would be wrong to use it the way you want me to.

ANNE. Monsenor, without your active support, this new government will fail.

HECTOR. Say nothing, Monsenor. I assure you nothing has changed.

ANNE. You have no choice, Monsenor. You must make a statement.

ROMERO. I already have.

HECTOR. What does that mean?

ANNE *(to HECTOR)*. He means he knew about the coup in advance. *(To ROMERO.)* Am I right?

ROMERO. I told them I will support those programs of theirs which in my judgment will help the people and oppose those programs which in my judgment will harm the people.

ANNE. That's not good enough, Monsenor. You need to make a public statement of support.

ROMERO. I am a spiritual leader, not a temporal ruler.

ANNE. You are responsible for the life of your people. You must do whatever is necessary for their well-being. Please don't hide behind vacuous distinctions.

HECTOR. Like Pontius Pilate, you're still trying to maintain your innocent neutrality. You cannot wash your hands of the blood that drenches this land. You must decide which side you are on. You must choose.

ROMERO. I have chosen! I have chosen the poor! You must understand me. I am telling you my life. Doesn't Matthew's Gospel teach us that Jesus rejected worldly power? When his disciples tried to make him a king to overthrow the Romans and set up an earthly kingdom, Jesus rebuked them. It is always a temptation to the Church to become a worldly kingdom.

HECTOR. We are a kingdom.

ANNE. Salvation starts here and now…

HECTOR. In history…

ANNE. In our flesh…

HECTOR. With our blood.

ANNE. Or it's just a lot of words! *(As HECTOR and ANNE speak the above lines they start to fade away. ROMERO turns away from them.)*

ROMERO. No! Salvation is the work of God, not of men. We are laborers in his vineyards. We do not know the fullness of his plans, the vastness of his estate. We do not see the results of our labor. We labor in faith.

(As ROMERO speaks these lines he moves to a place where he is alone, then suddenly he is surrounded by his brother BISHOPS. The BISHOPS chant the following accusations as if they were chanting a sacred litany. The NUNCIO acts as the leader of this liturgy. [Note: Some directors have opted to have the NUNCIO play all these lines. The NUNCIO then chants the BISHOPS' lines and speaks his in a normal manner.])

BISHOP. Your refusal to bless the new recruits…

BISHOP. …and new planes…

BISHOP. …was an insult to the heroic soldiers of our country.

ALL BISHOPS. We have written Rome of these things.

NUNCIO. Oscar, my son, we are at war. The Soviets know that the future will be won or lost here in the Third World. The United States has power and wealth, but no vision. It is a spiritually bankrupt nation. The Church is the only force in the world capable of saving the values of Western Civilization.

BISHOP. The new Pope understands this…

BISHOP. He has seen the horrors of atheistic materialism.

BISHOP. He knows the tyranny of socialist utopias.

NUNCIO. We must not be deceived by the rhetoric of human rights, the rhetoric of social justice.

BISHOP. We need the United States…

BISHOP. We need the Army…

BISHOP. We need the Oligarchy…

BISHOP. To stop the Hun.

BISHOP. To buy us time.

NUNCIO. Until we can defeat this evil force. We must stop the communists.

ALL BISHOPS. You are our general.

(ANNE and HECTOR become visible, add their voices to this litany of pressure on ROMERO to be what others want him to be for them.)

ANNE and HECTOR. You must choose, Monsenor.
ALL BISHOPS. You are our prince.
ANNE and HECTOR. You must decide.
ALL BISHOPS. You are St. Michael defending the Gates of Heaven.
ANNE and HECTOR. It is your duty to lead the people.
ROMERO *(breaking out of this circle of pressure, cries out).* No! I will choose who I will be.

SCENE TWO: The Price

Three weeks later. ANNE is working in the chancery.

HECTOR. The firing squads will be busy tonight.
ANNE. Shut up, Hector!
HECTOR. Out go the civilians and in come the generals just like I told him. In record time too!
ANNE. For God's sake, quit gloating. It's dreadful. They've petitioned Rome for his removal.
HECTOR. What are their chances?
ANNE. Good to very good. They've asked for an Apostolic Administrator to take charge of the diocese. His refusal to attend the inauguration of the new president was the last straw.
HECTOR. For an old woman, ah, excuse me, he does have courage.

ANNE. Their petition charges that he is emotionally and physically unfit.

HECTOR. Actually, his health has been perfect since he got knocked off his horse in Aguilares.

ANNE. They say, and I quote, that he is under the influence of certain notorious Marxist priests and foreign nuns.

HECTOR. I wish he were.

ANNE. Let's hope Rome acts in its customary snail-like manner. The people would never accept it. More bloodshed.

HECTOR. Inevitable.

ANNE. You certainly have a cavalier attitude toward death.

HECTOR. All progress involves blood.

ANNE. You Marxists are very lucky to have your dialectic. It so conveniently explains everything.

HECTOR. You have to de-structure things before you can re-structure them.

ANNE. And people?

HECTOR. Yes, people too. It's part of the historical process.

ANNE. Screw your historical process!

HECTOR. We are all involved in killing!

ANNE. No!

HECTOR. Not even in your heart? When those police in Mississippi beat you and left you naked on the side of a road, did you feel love for them?

ANNE. There's a big difference between wanting to kill someone and doing it.

HECTOR. Jesus said they were the same.

ANNE. Jesus was wrong!

HECTOR. My ancestors tore the hearts out of "volunteers" so that the Sun would rise again. People understand blood. Your civil rights movement in the states won respectability through nonviolent tactics, but it took the blood of Martin Luther King to touch people's hearts.

ANNE. Nonviolence is a spirituality! Not a tactic! Not a cloak you casually discard when you no longer need it! You're being cruel and cynical!

HECTOR. Neither! I'm just trying to understand. I'm trying to look at things objectively, Anne, not as I would like to see them. People are not moved by words. They like their martyrs. Look at Jesus on the Cross and understand the power of that symbol.

ANNE. When I look at the Cross, I see the incredible love Jesus had for us. That's what I see. Not a dialectic, not a symbol. I see a fact. Two facts: He loved me and we killed him. The tragedy is that it wasn't inevitable. Jesus didn't die to make us understand. It wasn't part of some strategy! We killed him because we failed to understand. His death is the result of our failure. Every time we kill it's the result of our failure, not part of some grand cosmic scheme. I don't want anyone to die. *(ANNE and HECTOR embrace.)*

SCENE THREE: The Rule of God

ROMERO is concluding a homily he is giving the Carmelite nuns.

ROMERO.

Happy are the poor, for theirs is the kingdom of God
Happy are they that mourn, for they are comforted
Happy are the meek, for theirs is the Earth
Happy are they who hunger and thirst after justice,
for they have found it
Happy are the merciful, for they have found mercy

Happy are the pure in heart, for they see God
Happy are the peacemakers, for they are the children of God

When Christ came down from the mountain, these were the new commandments he gave us. These were the articles of the new constitution of the people of God. My dear sisters, Matthew tells us very clearly whom God has chosen.

(As the lights go down on ROMERO, they go up on HECTOR who is at a meeting of STRIKE ORGANIZERS. ROMERO remains slightly visible in the background. GHANAN, ceremonially vested, appears at ROMERO's side.)

SCENE FOUR: The Understanding

HECTOR with the STRIKE ORGANIZERS at an unspecified place.

HECTOR *(speaks in Spanish then in English)*. Is everything ready?
ORGANIZER. Some of the unions are waiting to see what happens. We expect a compliance of about ninety percent.
HECTOR. What about security? This new president is out for blood.
ORGANIZER. I don't think they'll hit us the first day.
ORGANIZER. The death squads *(Spanish expletives.)* will try to hit the leaders at night.
ORGANIZER. We've set up a series of safe houses for them and their immediate families. Your friend, the Archbishop, is starting to see the light. Should I prepare a party card for him?

ORGANIZER. We could call him Red Bird One.
HECTOR. He's a good man.
ORGANIZER. A trifle naive politically.
HECTOR. He learns.

(Gunfire. A state of alarm ensues. HECTOR takes out a revolver which he had hidden on his person. ROMERO becomes more visible in the background. More gunfire. They all scatter. HECTOR fires his gun at the unseen enemy. HECTOR is shot. He falls to the floor, dies with the gun in his hand. ROMERO moves forward into the light, views the body and the gun in great horror. GHANAN honors the fallen warrior. The NUNCIO appears.)

NUNCIO. My dear, Oscar, let me assure you, you have my complete sympathy. Most unfortunate. A bit of friendly advice. I wouldn't give Hector a priestly burial. Rome wouldn't like that. It's not like the situation with Rutilio, not at all. Hector stepped across the line. When he picked up the gun he severed himself from the sacred bonds of the priesthood. You owe him nothing. "Those who live by the sword shall die by the sword." If you bury Hector, it will be a clear message to the people: the Church blessing a priest who took up arms against the lawful government...
ROMERO. We cannot judge him.
NUNCIO. We must. We are appointed by God to lead the people. We do not judge his soul. We judge his actions.
ROMERO. I reject violence. I reject guns.
NUNCIO. Good. Then it is settled?
ROMERO. Do you remember the play *Antigone*?
NUNCIO. How could I forget? Fr. Hermann made me translate every line of it.
ROMERO. She buried her brother.

NUNCIO. Those were noble times, Oscar, noble deeds, noble persons. Not like today.

ROMERO. Against King Creon's explicit command, she buried her brother.

NUNCIO. You are not his sister.

ROMERO. Not because she agreed with her brother's actions.

NUNCIO. You are not Antigone. You were Hector's commander, his prince.

ROMERO. I was his spiritual father, his friend.

NUNCIO. In this play, Oscar, you are Creon. Do not confuse your roles. He set aside personal feeling. He acted for the common good.

ROMERO. We cannot always calculate the good. Some things must be done simply because they are right. Whether I am Creon as you say or a prince as Hector wanted me to be, my first duty is to human dignity. The common good begins there, your Excellency, in one human being having respect for another. Whether I am his prince or his brother, I must bury him. *(ROMERO takes the body of HECTOR into his arms. The NUNCIO fades away.)* Lord, take to your bosom Hector, my son. Hector, my son! *(GHANAN hangs his great shield on the tomb monument being readied for ROMERO, takes the body of HECTOR from the arms of ROMERO.)*

SCENE FIVE: The Plea

(1)

Rapid scene change. ROMERO is in Washington, D.C. appearing before a Congressional Committee conducting hearings on aid To El Salvador. The GUARDIANS play the CON-

GRESSMEN. The CONGRESSMEN are not seen. They are VOICES from offstage.

CONGRESSMAN. Thank you, Monsenor, for coming all the way to Washington to testify before our committee. Let me begin by congratulating you on your recent nomination for the Nobel Peace Prize. We all read your letter to President Carter with great interest.

CONGRESSMAN. With all due respect, sir, we think you're underestimating the communist threat to your nation.

ROMERO. Anyone who opposes the Oligarchy of El Salvador is called a communist.

CONGRESSMAN. Your own bishops do not agree with your assessment of the situation. The president of your country calls you the rebel bishop.

ROMERO. If so, it's only because of my striking resemblance to James Dean. Gentlemen, do you have any questions that concern the poor of my country?

CONGRESSMAN. Sir, you cannot deny the existence of terrorist organizations that violently seek the overthrow of the legitimate government of your country.

ROMERO. The violence in El Salvador is the institutionalized violence of an unjust social system. That is the cause, directly or indirectly, of all the violence.

CONGRESSMAN. Sir, our intelligence reports clearly show that the guerrillas in your country are receiving aid from the Soviet Union through Cuba and Nicaragua.

ROMERO. Whatever military aid they receive, and I condemn such aid, is a mere trickle compared to the torrents of military aid your country gives the current government of El Salvador.

CONGRESSMAN. Do you in fact condone this rebellion against the legitimate government of El Salvador?

ROMERO. The Church does not call brother to rise against brother, or sister to rise against sister. But it does recognize the right of a people to defend the life of their community. The people have a right to take up arms against an evident and prolonged tyranny. The money and weapons you give the military of El Salvador are not used to fight the rebels. They are used to repress my people.

ALL CONGRESSMEN. If we don't continue our aid to your country, your country, like Cuba and Nicaragua, will fall under the influence of the Soviet Union and our vital interests will be—

ROMERO. The war in El Salvador is a war between those who want to grow their own rice and beans and those who hold the land by force against them. It is a war of your culture against our culture. To us there is no difference between a capitalist who takes our land and a Marxist who takes our land. I am not seeking progress. I am seeking justice. I am not seeking development. I am seeking justice. I am not choosing Marxism or capitalism. I am choosing justice. I beg you. I plead with you. It is our country. Let us develop in our own way, according to our own customs, according to our own insights. Please stop helping us. Please stop all aid to El Salvador. *(As ROMERO reaches the end of this statement, the GUARDIANS start to beat the ceremonial drums softly.)*

(2)

(While ANNE speaks, the GUARDIANS encircle ROMERO.)

ANNE. The whole village of Aguilares, Monsenor, every man, woman, and child.

ALL GUARDIANS *(softly)*. What will you do, Romero?

ANNE. Every dog and goat.

ALL GUARDIANS. What will you do, Romero? What will you do?

ANNE. Every pig and chicken. Every cat, every parrot, every turkey, every burro.

ALL GUARDIANS. First the road, then the soldiers.

ANNE. After they killed every living thing, they bulldozed the entire village. Every building, every structure. They tamped the debris down like the surface of a road. *(ANNE fades away. The GUARDIANS press ROMERO.)*

GUARDIAN. The blood of our children soaks the earth.

ROMERO. What can I do that I have not already done?!

GUARDIAN. Yours is the only voice left.

ROMERO. I have done all that is within my power!

GUARDIAN. Great demons possess the land.

GUARDIAN. Great demons devour the people.

ROMERO. What more can I do?!

GUARDIAN. You are the Exorcist.

GUARDIAN. You are the Appointed One.

ALL GUARDIANS. It is the Lord God who speaks: "This is what pleases me—to break unjust fetters and undo the chains of oppression, to free the poor and untie the ropes that bind them. Then, when you cry, Lord, Lord, I will say, Here I am."

GUARDIAN. The blood of Hector.

GUARDIAN. The blood of Rutilio.

GUARDIAN. The blood of Aguilares.

ROMERO. If it were just my life, mine alone.

SCENE SIX: The Confrontation/Reconciliation

(1)

The NUNCIO and the COLONEL.

COLONEL. He has gone too far.

NUNCIO. I have petitioned Rome for his removal, as you know.

COLONEL. That was months ago.

NUNCIO. Rome has the perspective of centuries, my dear Colonel, not of months.

COLONEL. We cannot wait.

NUNCIO. Our age is sorely lacking in many virtues, patience being one of them.

COLONEL. I did not come here to be lectured.

NUNCIO. Forgive an old man his habits.

COLONEL. In El Salvador, when a dog goes mad, we don't go to court and ask a judge for permission to kill it.

NUNCIO. A priest is one thing, Colonel, an archbishop is another.

COLONEL. The fate of the nation is at stake.

NUNCIO. And all that money from the United States.

COLONEL. The Americans have sent an emissary to the Vatican. Even they are sick of him. We have sent them a signal.

NUNCIO. I caution you. Living saints are much easier to handle than dead ones.

COLONEL. He is not a saint! He is not of God, but of Satan!

NUNCIO. In my experience, my dear Colonel, whether they be of heaven or of hell, the trouble they cause me is very nearly the same.

COLONEL. If you are not prepared to protect the Christian religion, then we will.

NUNCIO. We do what we can, Colonel. Some things are not for us to decide. "The Gates of Hell shall not prevail." That is Christ's promise to his Church.

COLONEL. When I want a sermon, Your Excellency, I go to church. One of the reasons I left your church was so that I could give my own sermons in my own church.

NUNCIO. Another tedious freedom of our times.

COLONEL. He must be stopped.

NUNCIO. On this we agree.

COLONEL. Good.

NUNCIO. In principle!

COLONEL. Why don't we let the unpleasant details settle themselves.

(The COLONEL fades away. The NUNCIO moves to another area of the stage where ROMERO becomes visible.)

(2)

(The NUNCIO and ROMERO in the chancery.)

NUNCIO. Oscar, let us set everything aside, everything. Let us talk as brothers, as fellow students of Fr. Hermann, students of the classics. These revolutionaries, they are children. They think that history begins with Karl Marx and ends with themselves. You and I, we have studied not only Karl Marx but Seneca and Plotinus. Who today reads Plotinus?! Look at what your Marxist friends did in Nicaragua. They called a meeting of all the Miskito Indian chiefs and then they left them waiting for a week. Without food, or shelter. No student of history could do that. No student of Fr. Hermann. We know that the code of hospitality is far more important than their class struggle or their idea of dialectical progress. Now they have an Indian rebellion on their hands. These alleged humanists. They don't even know what a human being is! They think that Zeus and Vishnu and Isis are fairy tales, childish stories! *(Beat.)* Oscar, the Oligarchs of El Salvador are idiots, but they are our first line of defense. How can you support these people, Oscar?! How can you support these revolutionaries who have no sense of history?!

ROMERO. I oppose the tyranny and injustice of this government.

NUNCIO. There is a parable, I forget which Gospel, of the woman whose house is possessed by a demon. "Beware," Jesus said, "lest while you sweep one demon out the front door, seven enter through the back."

ROMERO. Your Excellency, that last time we met you told me that I was Creon. Is it not the duty of the prince to make judgments, to choose from among those possibilities available to him what best promotes the life of the people?

NUNCIO. I am not speaking to the Archbishop of San Salvador. I am speaking to the man, Oscar Romero.

ROMERO. The man, Oscar Romero, has taken your advice. He is no longer himself. *(Understanding the significance of these words, the NUNCIO alters his attitude to a formal, ceremonial one. He delivers the following warning out of a sense of duty.)*

NUNCIO. Were I you, Oscar, I would not go so freely among the people.

ROMERO. If I fear to walk among the people, then they have tied my legs.

NUNCIO. Were I you I would not use church funds to support peasant organizations and credit unions.

ROMERO. If I fear to reach out to the poor, then they have tied my hands.

NUNCIO. Were I you I would no longer broadcast my Sunday sermons throughout the country.

ROMERO. If I become afraid to say what I believe, then they have tied my tongue. What else is left? *(The mood changes back to an informal one.)*

NUNCIO. You know, Oscar, I've noticed that your stomach doesn't seem to trouble you anymore.

ROMERO. Not since Aguilares.

NUNCIO. You look quite fit. It seems adversity suits you. I leave for the shore tomorrow, a long overdue rest. *(The NUNCIO starts to leave. ROMERO stops him.)*

ROMERO. Your Excellency, your blessing. Before you go, please, your blessing. *(The NUNCIO is first startled, then touched. He moves to ROMERO. ROMERO falls on his knees, receives the NUNCIO's blessing. The NUNCIO exits. ROMERO moves to his desk.)*

SCENE SEVEN: The Acceptance/Easter Mystery

March 22, 1980. The chancery. Late at night. ROMERO is working on his final sermon. Enter ANNE.

ANNE. May I come in?

ROMERO. You can't sleep either?

ANNE. I don't sleep anymore. I just wait till morning. *(Beat.)* Are you still working on your sermon?

ROMERO. Yes, it's almost finished.

ANNE. Do you want me to type it for you?

ROMERO. No, thank you. The typewritten page makes everything look so final. My handwriting allows room for the

Holy Spirit, especially when I can't read what I've written. *(Beat.)* How is your writing going?

ANNE. For months I haven't been able to write a word. Tonight I find myself writing volumes, to my father of all people.

ROMERO. You fight with him, Anne, because you love him.

ANNE. If you measure love by the quantity and quality of our arguments, we love each other a great deal. *(Beat.)* Monsenor, I'm going to leave. I don't understand, you see. How can I be an advisor if I don't understand?

ROMERO. I'm not sure I understand any more than you do.

ANNE. Of course you do. You belong here. This is your country and these are your people. It was the same with Hector and Rutilio. Even when you don't know, you understand.

ROMERO. An interesting distinction.

ANNE. A real one. I've done everything I can. We North Americans think we've got all the answers. We think that with a little more money and a little more know-how we'll be able to fix everything.

ROMERO. I need you, Anne, as a friend. You are a comfort to me.

ANNE. I wasn't meant to be a comforter. I have too many prickles, like my father.

ROMERO. So what do you do now? Go back to the States and become president of First National Bank in Chicago?

ANNE. I don't know what I'm going to do. At first, I thought I'd go to Guatemala, but I can't do that, not now. I don't have anything left to give, Monsenor. I've always believed that all anyone needs to bring to a situation is intelligence, compassion, and all the relevant facts...I was wrong.

ROMERO. What you brought to us is yourself, with all your virtues and all your limitations. That is a great gift, and it is right, entirely right.

ANNE. I'm too much my father's daughter: I want results.

ROMERO. I'm not very patient myself.

ANNE. Then you're a very good actor.

ROMERO. Well, you know how much I love the cinema. Perhaps I should have been a movie star. Ed Asner or Marlon Brando.

ANNE. Oh God, how I wish this were all make believe! In my movie, Monsenor, the land reform program would already be successfully in place, and after that the literacy and rural health programs, and after that I'd turn down the directorship of the World Bank and work anonymously with Mother Teresa in Calcutta, achieving both worldly success and sainthood in one fell swoop.

ROMERO. Sounds very exhausting. I'm glad you didn't write this role for me.

ANNE. I too was miscast. I really can't live without my hair dryer and expensive shampoos.

ROMERO. Anne, I'll miss you.

ANNE *(turns abruptly toward the audience in a Brechtian manner)*. We both understood I would not leave until it was over.

(The GUARDIANS appear in full ceremonial attire. ROMERO and ANNE progressively become removed from one another into their own worlds. The GUARDIANS gradually take full possession of ROMERO and prepare him for the sacrifice as the Fifth Sun.)

ROMERO. Tomorrow it all starts again. God's great cosmic drama in which we all play our proper roles. The eternal cycle of life, death, and resurrection. What magnificent poetry! I became a priest because of the beauty and power of Holy Week.

ANNE. I won't embrace death, Monsenor. I won't cover death with lilies.

GUARDIANS. Is the message to our people ready?

ROMERO. Yes, my Lords. *(As each GUARDIAN speaks to ROMERO, they each embrace him in turn.)*

KUKULCAN. Thou art Nanautzin, our brother.

GHANAN. Thou art the Lamb of God.

CHAC. Thou art the Center.

AHPUCH. Thou art *The Fifth Sun,* the Sun of the People!

(The GUARDIANS begin to vest ROMERO for the mass/sacrifice. They chant either singly or in unison as they vest him).

GUARDIANS.

- And the Word created the World and all things in it.
- And the Word asked his sons: Which one of you will light the World and give it life?
- And none was willing for each knew the price.
- Though he was in the form of God he cherished it not.
- Nanautzin came forward and said: In compassion for all the World, let it be according to your Word.
- For nine days and nights he fasted and prayed.
- In him was life and the life was the light of the World.
- Nanautzin climbed the great temple, gathered his courage...

(ROMERO takes his crozier, moves to the place where he is to deliver his last sermon. The sermon is being broadcast over the Archdiocesan radio station.)

ROMERO. We thank God for those who work to keep our poor radio station alive. We know the great risk they take every day to be the voice of an entire people that seeks for truth and justice. We give thanks to God for this marvelous means of communication that unites us, that allows us to share our sufferings, the preparation for our Easter.

My brothers and sisters, no one can extinguish the life which Christ restored to us by his death. As Christ flourishes in an Easter unending, it is necessary that we accompany him now in Lent, in a Holy Week that is cross, sacrifice, martyrdom.

I know that many of you are shocked by my relating the Gospel to the political situation in our country. You accuse me of meddling in politics, of abandoning my proper role as bishop. Some of you even accuse me of being the Anti-Christ because I see and accept the political consequences of the Gospel. I do not accept your accusation. I do not accept your version of Christianity.

During the whole week as I go about our sorrowing nation gathering up the cries of the people, the aches of so much ignominy, I ask the Lord to give me the suitable word: To Console, To Denounce, To Call to Repentance. And even if I am left alone, a voice crying in the wilderness, I shall not shut my mouth. I am the pastor. I will sound my voice over the land.

This past week in Aguilares we celebrated the third anniversary of the assassination of Fr. Rutilio Grande. Yes, even in that village martyred in the extreme, Life is returning. Life is coming back! They could not kill Rutilio. They could not kill Aguilares!

I have warned the rich time and time again to open their hearts, to open their hands, to give away their fancy rings, because if they don't, the time will soon come when these glittering signs of their exploitation of the poor will be cut off.

The death and destruction that everywhere engulfs our poor nation is caused by a small group of families who don't care about the hunger of the people. When anyone raises his voice against them, they kill him. I praise Rutilio Grande, Alfonso Navarro, Octavio Ortiz, Ernesto Barrera, Hector Navarez. Yes, I praise Fr. Hector Navarez. We Christians prefer the language of peace, but we are not afraid of combat. We know how to fight when it becomes necessary to defend the life of the people!

I want now to address a special word to the men in the army, to the soldiers of the National Guard, to the police: Brothers, you belong to our own people. You are one of us. You are killing your own brothers and sisters, your own campesinos and Indians. In the face of an order to kill, obey the greater law of God which clearly says: THOU SHALT NOT KILL! I say to you as your teacher and pastor: No soldier is obliged to obey an order counter to the law of God. No one has to comply with an immoral law. It is time now for you to recover your conscience and obey its dictates rather than the sinful commands of men. The Church cannot remain silent before so much abomination. Therefore, in the name of God, and in the name of your own long-suffering people, whose cries rise to heaven every day more tumultuously, I beseech you, I beg you, I command you in the name of God: *cease the repression!*

(When ROMERO utters the words "cease the repression" the ceremonial drums commence their ritual beat. The GUARDIANS lead ROMERO to the altar where he continues with the mass, preparing the bread and wine for consecration. The GUARDIANS take their proper positions at the four corners of the cosmic altar with ROMERO in the center.)

ROMERO. Sisters and brothers, pray that our sacrifice might be acceptable to God.

GUARDIANS. May the Lord accept the sacrifice at your hands for the praise and glory of his name, for our good, and the good of all God's people.

ROMERO. Lord, hear the prayers of your people. May you see in this sacrifice which we now offer you the fullness of our faith and love. The Lord be with you.

GUARDIANS. And also with you.

ROMERO. Lift up your hearts.

GUARDIANS. With joy we lift them up to the Lord.

(As ROMERO says the sacred words of consecration, a WHITE WARRIOR OF CHRIST, dressed impeccably in an immaculate business suit, emerges from the rear of the theater in the audience. He wears a white mask and white gloves and carries a M-16 rifle which he aims at ROMERO's heart. The drums start to beat.)

ROMERO. Before he was given up to Death, a Death which he freely accepted, he took bread and gave thanks. He broke the bread, gave it to his disciples and said: Take this, all of you, and eat. This is my Body which I give to you. Happy are they who are called to this Feast. Then, he took the cup, again he gave thanks and praise. Take this cup all of you, and drink of it. This is my Blood which I give to you. Happy are they who are called...

(With these words, the WHITE WARRIOR shoots. ROMERO falls dead over the altar. The drums beat wildly and the cymbals clang. The GUARDIANS take the body of ROMERO and place it on the altar to complete the Mayan ritual of this sacrifice. AHPUCH sets in place the last great shield of death, completing the tomb monument.)

GUARDIANS *(individually or in unison).*

- Unto all ages
- Unto all ages is given a Sun
- Unto all ages
- Unto all ages a Guardian

ANNE. On the day of his funeral, the people of El Salvador erected a great banner over the door of the Cathedral. This banner prohibited all the bishops of El Salvador, except one, from attending the funeral. The people excommunicated these bishops and all those who refused to work for Justice...*(When ANNE speaks this last line, the GUARDIANS break a large candle and spill the sacred wine.)*...After they murdered him, the chancery was bombed and destroyed.

GUARDIANS. In every age the call is made

ANNE. Our radio station was bombed and destroyed.

GUARDIANS. In every age the sacrifice

ANNE. The Jesuit House of Studies was bombed and destroyed.

GUARDIANS. To give light

ANNE. The House of the Belgium Fathers was bombed and destroyed.

GUARDIANS. To give life

ANNE. Thirty-seven parishes were violated by the National Guard who tore open the tabernacles and defecated on the sacred hosts.

GUARDIANS. We are the Bacab Balam

ANNE. On October 7, 1980, Fr. Manuel Reyes was murdered, the eleventh priest in three years.

GUARDIANS. We are the guardian spirits

ANNE. On December 2, 1980, they assassinated my friends: *(After each name the GUARDIANS chant—Presente!)*

- Sr. Maura Clarke of Maryknoll
- Sr. Ita Ford of Maryknoll
- Sr. Dorothy Kazel of the Ursulines
- Miss Jean Donovan, lay missioner

GUARDIANS.

We are the Bacab Balam
We are the guardians of this land

ANNE. Happy are they who are called…

GUARDIANS. To us was entrusted the care of the peoples:

- of Chiapas
- of the Yucatan
- of Guatemala
- of Honduras
- of El Salvador

ALL. All hail the New Sun!

ANNE. Oscar Arnulfo Romero!

ALL. Presente!

THE END

PRODUCTION NOTES

STAGING AREA:

The ruins of an ancient temple with the symbols of the Catholic and Mayan religions co-existing in creative tension. The space should have a quality that transcends time and space and should facilitate the rapid, iconographic transitions required by the script.

Because *THE FIFTH SUN* is constructed as a tomb/ritual drama, it should be performed with music and dance. The Guardians play primitive musical instruments, dance, and sing ritual chant to enhance and to develop the dramatic presentation.

Kukulcan, Ahpuch, Chac, and Ghanan are the four compass points or suns of the Mayan/Nahuatlan cosmos. They also function as the elemental forces and protectors of the Indian world. The fifth sun, the sun of the people, stands at the center of the cosmic grid. Each Guardian has a distinctive mask/headdress which represents his special function in creation. Each is robed and painted in his cosmic color: Ahpuch (white), Ghanan (red), Chac (blue), Kukulcan (black). Gold is reserved for the fifth sun. The Guardians may be played by either men or women.

The actors playing the Guardians also play the bishops, the villagers, the strike organizers, and other roles according to the physical possibilities inherent in the script and the requirements of the particular production. In the Victory Gardens production in Chicago, the actor who played KUKULCAN also played THE NUNCIO, the actor who played GHANAN also played THE COLONEL, and the actor who played RUTILIO GRANDE also played THE ASSASSIN. In The Group production in Seattle, which enjoyed the advantage of having professional dancers playing the Guardians, none of the principal roles was doubled. In the Black Ensemble production at St. Louis University, each Guardian was played by a chorus of actors to emphasize the poetic/vocal qualities of these roles.

The ensemble version of THE FIFTH SUN was developed in a series of workshops beginning in the spring of 1988 with the Latino Chicago Theater Company and concluding in the winter of 1990 with the Commons Theatre Company in Chicago. This ensemble version is available in typescript form by applying to the publishers.

CHARACTERS:

OSCAR ROMERO is a native Salvadoran man in his sixties and appears dressed in a plain black Roman cassock with modest purple piping. He wears a plain wooden crucifix around his neck and black rimmed glasses. He is an earthy man with a teasing sense of humor. He is a "mestizo," a Salvadoran of mixed white and Indian blood. Romero moved to a position of "solidarity with the poor" from a traditionalist, even pietistic, spirituality. He was judged to be a weak and sickly man by all sides prior to his installation. To the astonishment of all, he grew physically and emotionally stronger as the burdens of his office grew greater.

ANNE DUNN is a native of the USA, a woman in her late thirties and appears dressed in proper and neat civilian clothes. She is a highly intelligent and competent person, with a strong drive to succeed. She holds a Ph.D. in economics from the University of Chicago and worked with the AFL/CIO union organizing and land reform projects in El Salvador before joining the Archdiocesan staff. Anne is a pragmatist and a questioning believer.

HECTOR NAVAREZ is a native-born Salvadoran man in his late twenties and appears in standard working-class clothes. He is of Indian blood, recently ordained, and is passionately committed to making the Catholic Church a revolutionary force on the side of the poor.

RUTILIO GRANDE is a native-born Salvadoran man in his fifties and appears dressed in a plain black Jesuit cassock. A seminary professor for twenty years, he left his "ivory tower" to become pastor of Aguilares and learn about God from the life of the poor.

THE NUNCIO is a Spaniard in his early seventies and appears dressed in an ornate Roman cassock with red sash and piping, red skull cap, and a gold crucifix around his neck. He is a career diplomat.

THE COLONEL is a native Salvadoran man in his early forties and appears impeccably dressed in an officer's uniform. He is a member of the upper class and fanatically dedicated to preserving the status quo.

THE ASSASSIN is a White Warrior of Christ and appears dressed in a business suit with a white hood over his head and a USA-type military rifle in his hands.

Glossary

AHPUCH: (Ah-pooch) god of death, north.
CHAC: (Schahk) god of rain, south.
GHANAN: (Ga-nahn) god of maize or cultivation, east.
KUKULCAN: (Coo-cool-cahn) god of life, west.
BACAB BALAM: (Ba-cahb Ba-lahm) four gods of the cosmic grid.
NANAUTZIN: (Na-now-tseen) son of the lord of creation who willingly sacrifices himself to become the fifth sun, the sun of our world.

(All the above Mayan words are accented on the last syllable; the vowel "a" is sounded like the broad "a" in "father.")

THE MATANZA: "The massacre." In 1932, 30,000 Indians and peasants were slaughtered, allegedly to thwart a communist insurrection against the landowners. This massacre virtually wiped out Indian life in El Salvador.

MEDELLIN CONFERENCE: In 1968, the Latin American Bishops Conference met in Medellin, Colombia and declared the Catholic Church to be on the side of the poor. At this same conference, Pope Paul VI proclaimed the right of a people to employ the force of arms to overthrow "an evident and prolonged tyranny."

ORDEN: A paramilitary force organized in the '60s to police the campesinos of the El Salvadoran countryside. The members of ORDEN were so brutal that this organization was officially suppressed after the coup of 1979.

FPL: Popular Liberation Forces, the most powerful of the three main guerrilla groups. It forcefully opposed ORDEN in the countryside and union-busters in the cities.

PLAZA LIBERTAD MASSACRE: In 1977, five days after the installation of Monsenor Romero, thousands marched to Plaza Libertad to protest the fraudulent election of General Romero (no relation to the Monsenor). Several hundred demonstrators were killed when the police and army opened fire on them. Two thousand took refuge in Rosario Church and were saved through the intervention of Monsenor Chavez, the retired Archbishop of San Salvador.

FR. RUTILIO GRANDE: A Jesuit priest and close friend of Monsenor Romero. He and his two companions, Nelson and Manuel, were assassinated three weeks after the massacre in Plaza Libertad. Fr. Rutilio's death was the first of many assassinations of nuns, priests, and religious lay workers. Fr. Grande left his seminary professorship to become pastor of Aguilares, a village outside of San Salvador. In Aguilares, Fr. Grande established the first "base community" in El Salvador.

WHITE WARRIORS: A vigilante group which vowed to kill the remaining forty-seven Jesuits in El Salvador and all foreign or "Marxist" religious workers.

BASE COMMUNITIES: *(comunidades de base)* a grass-roots movement among the Catholic poor based on the pedagogy of the oppressed by Paulo Freire. This movement began in Brazil where there are currently 70,000 such communities. The members of these communities teach themselves to read and write and to meet their own "basic" needs without having to rely on corrupt or inefficient social institutions.

Select Bibliography

The Word Remains: A Life of Oscar Romero. James R. Brockman. Orbis Books, Maryknoll, NY. 1982.

Cry Of The People. Penny Lernoux. Doubleday, Garden City, NY. 1980.

Salvador Witness: The Life And Calling Of Jean Donovan. Ana Carrigan. Simon and Schuster, New York, NY. 1984.

Weakness And Deceit: U.S. Policy And El Salvador. Raymond Bonner. Times Books, New York, NY. 1984.

Chronology

1977

February 3	Monsenor Luis Chavez y Gonzalez resigns as Archbishop of San Salvador.
February 20	General Carlos Humberto Romero elected president in an election judged fraudulent by most observers.
February 22	Monsenor Oscar Arnulfo Romero installed as Archbishop of San Salvador.
February 24	Colonel Ernesto Claramount, a retired cavalry officer, begins a demonstration/vigil in Plaza Libertad to protest the massive fraud by the government in the general elections.
February 27	The army opens fire on the demonstrators in Plaza Libertad, killing or arresting (never to be seen again) between 80 and 300 people. Around 2,000 people seek sanctuary in Rosario Church which adjoins the square. Only the intervention of Monsenor Chavez saves them from the slaughter.
March 12	Rutilio Grande, S.J., and his two companions, Nelson and Manuel, are assassinated on their way to El Paisnal, a mission parish in the mountains. Although many priests had been arrested and tortured prior to Fr. Grande's death, this is the first time a priest

or a religious has been murdered in El Salvador. This assassination of a religious is the first of many which continue to this day.

March 14 Monsenor Romero excommunicates those responsible for the murder of Fr. Grande and his companions and he informs the outgoing President Arturo Molina that the Church will not cooperate with the government until it brings the murderers to justice.

March 26 Monsenor Romero goes to Rome to explain personally to the Pope (Paul VI) and to the Curia his actions in response to the murder of Fr. Rutilio Grande. This trip was made necessary because of the opposition of the Papal Nuncio who had denounced Romero's conduct.

May 11 Four White Warriors murder Fr. Alfonso Navarro and his fifteen-year-old companion, Luis Torres.

May 17 The first massacre of Aguilares takes place. Over fifty peasants are killed by the army. Three Jesuit priests are arrested and expelled.

May 18 Monsenor Romero tries to go to Aguilares but the National Guard will not let him through. The National Guard desecrates the village church.

June 19 — Monsenor Romero goes to Aguilares to celebrate the restoration of the parish church and to install the new pastor.

June 21 — The White Warriors warn all Jesuits to leave El Salvador within 30 days, after which they and their institutions would become "military targets."

July 1 — Monsenor Romero refuses to attend the inauguration of the new president, General Carlos Humberto Romero (no relation).

July 11-13 — The El Salvadoran bishops meet as a group to discuss policy issues. In general, the bishops, except for one, and the Nuncio disagree with Romero's policies and actions.

July 21 — The deadline the White Warriors had given the Jesuits to leave El Salvador "or else."

United States House Sub-Committee on International Organizations holds hearings on religious persecutions in El Salvador.

August 10 — Monsenor Romero meets with President Romero to "reach an understanding." This effort fails.

August 15 — Monsenor Romero's birthday. The official opening of the chancery "snack bar" which he championed.

August 21	Monsenor Romero visits Aguilares again to consecrate the new tabernacle which had been desecrated by the National Guard.
August 26	National Guard and Treasury Police attack catechists in the rural areas, killing and kidnapping them. Romero visits the attacked villages and the families of those killed or "disappeared."
October	Bishop Revelo, El Salvador's delegate to Bishops' Synod in Rome, charges that the best and brightest rural catechists are Marxists or under Marxist influence. Monsenor Romero writes Revelo and the Nuncio letters to protest this charge.
November	*La Opinion* and *La Prensa Grafica* print many articles accusing Romero of being a Marxist and of supporting violence. In general, the press of El Salvador carry many articles and advertisements seeking to discredit Romero.
December 1	Monsenor Romero says mass for the mothers of the thousands of "disappeared" persons. He tells them that to denounce injustice is not meddling in politics, but an act of faith against sin.

1978

January	Monsenor Romero holds a three-day conference on peace and justice. The clergy and religious of the archdiocese release a statement announcing their support of Romero to counter the opposition of the Nuncio and the bishops (except for Bishop Rivera y Damas, Romero's lone supporter).
February 14	Georgetown University bestows an honorary degree on Romero for his work for peace and human rights.
March	Three hundred clergy and religious sign a letter which censures the Nuncio's (Emmanuele Gerada) conduct.
April	Bishops Aparicio, Barrera, Alvarez, and Revelo publish a letter in support of the Nuncio. Aparicio publicly accuses Romero of "dividing and confusing" the nation.
March/April	ORDEN, a para-military organization based in the countryside, launches a series of attacks on peasant organizations. Romero offers refugee peasants sanctuary in the chancery and in the seminary for which he is censured by some of the bishops.
April 30	Romero denounces the judiciary of El Salvador for not protecting human rights and for not

bringing to justice those responsible for the criminal activities of the security forces.

May	Romero again ordered to Rome to explain himself. He writes a long report to Cardinal Biaggi before going to Rome.
June	Romero goes to Rome, meets with Biaggi and Pope Paul VI. The Pope continues to support Romero over the opposition of the Curia and the Nuncio.
August	Romero issues a pastoral letter recognizing the right of peasants to organize and seek their rights. This letter also recognizes the right of a people to use force in protecting themselves against "an evident and prolonged tyranny that seriously attacks the fundamental rights of the person and dangerously harms the common good..."
August 6	Pope Paul VI dies suddenly. The Nuncio, Cardinal Casariego of Guatemala, and President Romero seek to have Monsenor Romero removed from office.
September	John Paul I dies "mysteriously."
October 16	John Paul II becomes Pope.
November	Monsenor Romero nominated by British Parliament for the Nobel Peace Prize.

November 28 Fr. Ernesto "Neto" Barrera, a young priest who worked with labor unions, is killed along with four members of the FPL in a shoot-out with security forces.

December Romero decides to give Fr. Barrera a priestly burial even though there is evidence he was a member of the FPL.

December Bishop Antonio Quarracino of Avellaneda, Argentina, is appointed Apostolic Visitor to San Salvador and investigates Monsenor Romero. He recommends to Rome that an Apostolic Administrator be named to rule the archdiocese, leaving Romero only in charge of strictly religious duties.

1979

January 20 Fr. Octavio Ortiz, and four young men, are killed by the police who attack some thirty young people on retreat at the diocesan retreat center. The government maintained this retreat was a clandestine meeting of subversives. In his homily, Romero calls the government's account of this incident "a lie from beginning to end."

January 22 Monsenor Romero goes to the Latin American Bishops' Conference in Puebla, Mexico. The Pope had appointed him an extraordinary delegate to this conference to represent the *communidades de base* of all Latin

America. The El Salvadoran bishops had refused to elect him to be their representative to this conference.

April/May — Romero goes to Rome again where Pope John Paul informs him that Bishop Quarracino had recommended that an Apostolic Administrator be named to govern the Archdiocese of San Salvador. In Rome, Romero also discovers a document sent to Rome by Bishops Aparicio, Alvarez, Barrera, and Revelo in which they accuse Romero of being a Marxist and Rutilio Grande of being a leftist terrorist.

May 1 — The government illegally arrests five leaders of an opposition labor party. Members of the party occupy the cathedral to protest these arrests.

May 8 — Security forces open fire on a small group of demonstrators in front of the cathedral. Twenty-five are killed, seventy are wounded. This event was recorded by international TV crews which were covering the demonstration.

May 22 — Security forces open fire on another small group of demonstrators, killing fourteen.

June 20 — The White Warriors kill Fr. Rafael Palacios.

July 19 — The Sandinistas overthrow Somoza in Nicaragua. Romero publicly expresses his joy over Somoza's ouster.

July 22 — In his homily, Romero speaks of the proper role of Christians in revolution and social change, using Nicaragua as an example.

August 6 — Romero issues his fourth pastoral letter in which he again recognizes the right of a people to use force when there is no other remedy. He also distinguishes between Marxism as an ideology which he condemns and Marxism as a tool of social and economic analysis which ought to be judged by its demonstrated merits. Further, he repeats that the Church equally condemns the sins of liberal capitalism as well as those of Marxism. He says: "The fear of Marxism keeps many from confronting the oppressive reality of liberal capitalism."

September — Romero receives a crude death threat from the White Warriors. He sends the threat to the Minister of Defense. Several churches are occupied by various popular organizations seeking justice.

October 7 — Romero's friend, Apolinaro Serrano, a peasant leader, is assassinated along with several other peasants. Romero is secretly approached by a group of reform-minded colonels who seek his support and advice concerning their plot to oust General Romero. Romero offers advice but refuses to endorse a coup.

October 14 In his Sunday homily which is always broadcast throughout El Salvador via the archdiocesan radio station YSAX, Romero lists the deeds of General Romero's government, concluding: "This government has emptied the prisons of political prisoners only to fill the cemeteries with the dead."

October 15 With U.S. support, the coup against General Romero is successful. The reform-minded colonels set-up a military/civilian junta to run the country. This junta, on paper, represents the first break in military rule of El Salvador since 1932.

Many observers consider this coup to be the most important event in the modern history of El Salvador. They see it as the first genuine opportunity for a truly democratic, coalition government.

November During the three weeks following the coup, the progressive military officers swiftly lost control of their own coup to the very generals they had sought to remove. Thus, their efforts to eliminate corruption, control the death squads, and establish a civilian government were entirely defeated. In fact, more innocent civilians were killed under this civilian government than under the military government of General Romero.

December 19 Leftist militants seize the chancery and other archdiocesan offices to protest Romero's support of the junta.

December 28 The civilian members of the junta resign to protest the murder and repression of workers, peasants, and religious. The Christian democrats decide to form a new junta with the military.

1980

January The Christian democrats try to organize a new government. They fail to attract capable civilian leaders and they fail to get the military to keep its promises concerning reform and control of the death squads.

January 6 In his Sunday homily, Romero praises those civilians who resigned from the junta and asks the military members to resign as well, especially colonel Jose Guillermo Garcia who was closely identified with the death squads.

January For the first time, the various groups and organizations opposed to government repression united in a broad coalition which included Christian democrats as well as communists. Also, two of the three armed resistance groups agree to join forces.

January 13, 20 Romero analyzes the political options for El Salvador in his Sunday homilies. He sees little hope in the military or in the Oligarchy. He praises the efforts of those popular organizations seeking to create unity among the various groups of the left. He concludes his analysis with an appeal to all groups to avoid civil war and to achieve justice.

January 22 To commemorate the anniversary of the peasant uprising of 1932 in which 30,000 Indians and campesinos were massacred, and to celebrate the growing unity among the various popular organizations, 200,000 marched to Plaza Libertad where once again they were attacked. Twenty-four were killed and 120 wounded.

January 30 Romero again goes to Rome to explain his actions personally to John Paul II. Romero feels that John Paul understands and approves of his handling of the situation.

February 2 Romero makes a major address at Louvain University in which he speaks on the political implications of the Catholic faith and the duty of the Church to stand in solidarity with the poor.

February 17 During his Sunday homily, Romero denounces the criminal elements of the military, calls upon the Christian democrats to leave the government, and reads a letter he has drafted to

President Carter asking him to stop all aid to El Salvador and to end all economic and diplomatic intervention in El Salvador and to "respect the legitimate self-determination of our people."

March 3 — Christian democrats resign from the government. A third junta is formed.

March 6 — The new junta announces a new land reform program which is opposed by the peasants. The new junta declares a state of siege and attacks all peasant organizations and cooperatives.

March — The White Warriors begin a massive campaign against Romero and the clergy who support the peasants. Roberto D'Aubuisson, the charismatic and fanatic leader of the ultra-rightist ARENA party, goes on national TV to deliver a harangue against Romero. He lectures a portrait of Romero whom he accuses of being a Marxist and an agent of the devil. Many observers link D'Aubuisson to the murder of Romero. There are witnesses who maintain that he and his associates drew straws for the honor of assassinating Romero.

March 23 — In his Sunday homily, Romero denounces the government's land reform program which the people resist with their blood and calls upon the National Guard and the other security forces to cease using their weapons against their own people.

March 24 Romero is assassinated while saying mass for the Carmelite nuns in the chapel in the hospital where he lives. Witnesses say he saw the assassin just before he shot him and that he forgave him.

March 30 Eighty-thousand people defy the government and attend Romero's funeral. The security forces open fire on the people, killing forty and wounding hundreds.

April 2 Despite Romero's letter and his assassination, both President Carter and the U.S. Congress approve more military aid to El Salvador.

April 8 Most of the popular organizations unite to form a united political opposition to the government. It is called the Democratic Revolutionary Front (FDR) and includes communists as well as Christian democrats, small businessmen as well as teachers and industrial workers.

May 4 Six hundred peasants, mostly women and children, are massacred by Salvadoran and Honduran troops as they try to cross the Sumpul River to escape marauding government troops indiscriminately killing all peasants. The brutality of this massacre shocks many hard-bitten, seasoned reporters.

June 24 Army occupies the National University, killing fifty. The university never re-opens.

August 12	Government bombs a section of San Salvador, killing two hundred.
September	U.S. increases military aid to El Salvador.
October	Army increases its war against the peasants. Archbishop Rivera y Damas, Romero's successor, denounces this "war of extermination" against the people.
November 11	The U.S. Bishops' Catholic Conference publicly opposes military aid to El Salvador.
November 19	The army attacks the archdiocesan newspaper offices and the radio station.
November 27	The army invades a Jesuit high school and arrests six members of the FDR Executive Committee who were meeting with archdiocesan officials at their request. All six were tortured, then murdered.
December 4	The bodies of four U.S. women, three nuns and one lay woman, are found. They had been raped, strangled, and shot by government security forces.
December 6	Archbishop Rivera asks the U.S. to stop all military aid to El Salvador, rejects the U.S. idea that the military junta represents the responsible political center. He says the junta represents the ultra-right and is responsible for the killings and the repression.

ARCHBISHOP ROMERO'S OPEN LETTER TO PRESIDENT CARTER

February 18, 1980

In the last few days, news has appeared in the national press that worries me greatly. According to the reports, your government is studying the possibility of economic and military support and assistance to the present junta government.

Because you are a Christian and because you have shown that you want to defend human rights, I venture to set forth for you my pastoral point of view concerning this news and to make a request.

I am very worried by the news that the government of the United States is studying a form of abetting the arming of El Salvador by sending military teams and advisors to "train three Salvadoran battalions in logistics, communications and intelligence." If this information from the newspapers is correct, the contribution of your government, instead of promoting greater justice and peace in El Salvador, will without doubt sharpen the injustice and repression against the organizations of the people who repeatedly have been struggling to gain respect for their most fundamental human rights.

The present junta government, and above all the armed forces and security forces, unfortunately have not demonstrated their capacity to resolve, in political and structural practice, the grave national problems. In general they have only reverted to repressive violence, producing a total of deaths and injuries much greater than in the recent military regimes whose systematic violation of human rights was denounced by the Inter-American Committee on Human Rights.

The brutal form in which the security forces recently attacked and assassinated the occupiers of the headquarters of the Christian Democratic Party in spite of what appears to be the lack of authorization for this operation from the junta government and the party is an indication that the junta and the party do not govern the country, but that political power is in the hands of the unscrupulous military who only know how to repress the people and promote the interests of the Salvadoran oligarchy.

If it is true that last November "a group of six Americans were in El Salvador...providing $200,000 in gas masks and flak jackets and instructing about their use against demonstrators," you yourself should be informed that it is evident since then that the security forces, with better personal protection and efficiency, have repressed the people even more violently using lethal weapons.

For this reason, given that as a Salvadoran and as archbishop of the Archdiocese of San Salvador I have an obligation to see that faith and justice reign in my country, I ask you, if you truly want to defend human rights, to prohibit the giving of this military aid to the Salvadoran government. Guarantee that your government will not intervene directly or indirectly with military, economic, diplomatic or other pressures to determine the destiny of the Salvadoran people.

In these moments we are living through a grave economic and political crisis in our country, but it is certain that it is increasingly the people who are awakening and organizing and have begun to prepare themselves to manage and be responsible for the future of El Salvador. Only they are capable of overcoming the crisis.

It would be unjust and deplorable if the intrusion of foreign powers were to frustrate the Salvadoran people, were to repress them and block their autonomous decisions about the economic and political path that our country ought to follow. It would violate a right which we Latin American bishops meeting in Puebla publicly recognized when we said: "The legitimate self-determination of our people that permits them to organize according to their own genius and the march of their history and to cooperate in a new international order."

I hope that your religious sentiments and your feelings for the defense of human rights will move you to accept my petition, avoiding by this action worse bloodshed in this suffering country.

DIRECTOR'S NOTES

DIRECTOR'S NOTES

DIRECTOR'S NOTES

DIRECTOR'S NOTES

DIRECTOR'S NOTES

DIRECTOR'S NOTES